Saber-Toothed Tiger

by Julie Murray

Abdo Kids Jumbo is an Imprint of Abdo Kids
abdobooks.com

abdobooks.com

Published by Abdo Kids, a division of ABDO, P.O. Box 398166, Minneapolis, Minnesota 55439.

Abdo Kids Jumbo™ is a trademark and logo of Abdo Kids.

Printed in the United States of America, North Mankato, Minnesota.

052023

092023

Photo Credits: Alamy, Getty Images, Science Source, Shutterstock, ©Roman Uchytel p.19

Production Contributors: Teddy Borth, Jennie Forsberg, Grace Hansen
Design Contributors: Candice Keimig, Pakou Moua

Library of Congress Control Number: 2022946803

Publisher's Cataloging-in-Publication Data

Names: Murray, Julie, author.

Title: Saber-toothed tiger / by Julie Murray

Description: Minneapolis, Minnesota : Abdo Kids, 2024 | Series: Ice age animals | Includes online resources and index.

Identifiers: ISBN 9781098266363 (lib. bdg.) | ISBN 9781098267063 (ebook) | ISBN 9781098267414 (Read-to-me ebook)

Subjects: LCSH: Animals--Juvenile literature. | Extinct animals--Juvenile literature. | Ice Age--Juvenile literature. | Paleontology--Juvenile literature. | Zoology--Juvenile literature.

Classification: DDC 569--dc23

Table of Contents

Ice Age 4

Saber-Toothed Tiger 6

Food 16

Extinction 20

More Facts 22

Glossary 23

Index 24

Abdo Kids Code. 24

Ice Age

An ice age is a period when most of the Earth is covered by sheets of ice. The last ice age began about 100,000 years ago. It lasted until about 12,000 years ago. Some animals became **extinct** during this time in history.

ice
land

Saber-Toothed Tiger

The saber-toothed tiger appeared more than 2.5 million years ago. It lived in North and South America. It was found in woodland and grassland areas.

North America
Europe
Asia
Africa
South America
N
E
S
W

The saber-toothed tiger was a large **predator** with thick fur. It stood 3 feet (0.9 m) tall at the shoulder. It could weigh more than 600 pounds (272 kg)!

The saber-toothed tiger had a muscular body. Its legs were short, but strong. It could run up to 30 miles per hour (48.3 kph).

Its large mouth could open wide to roar loudly. The saber-toothed tiger also had two giant canine teeth. The teeth were curved and could grow 8 inches long (20.3 cm)!

canine
tooth

The saber-toothed tiger had large paws. Its **retractable** claws were long and sharp.

Food

Saber-toothed tigers lived and hunted in groups. They were **ambush** hunters. They hid and waited before pouncing on their **prey**.

Saber-toothed tigers hunted animals such as horses, bison, and mammoths. Their paws and claws helped them hold onto their **prey**. Their large teeth helped finish the job.

Extinction

The saber-toothed tiger went **extinct** about 11,500 years ago. It was overhunted by humans. It also had trouble finding food to eat.

More Facts

- Even though it is called a tiger, it is not closely related to the tiger or other modern cats.
- Saber-toothed tigers probably lived 20 to 40 years.
- There were 35 **species** of saber-toothed cats. *Smilodon*, or saber-toothed tiger, was the biggest.
- Many of its **fossils** have been found in La Brea Tar Pits in Los Angeles, California. Because of this, it is the official state fossil of California.

Glossary

ambush – to make a surprise attack from a hidden place.

extinct – no longer existing.

fossil – the remains or trace of a living animal or plant from a long time ago.

predator – an animal that hunts other animals for food.

prey – an animal that is hunted by other animals for food.

retractable – able to be pulled back in.

species – a group of living things that look alike and can have young together.

Index

body 10

claws 14, 18

food 18, 20

fur 8

habitat 6

hunting 16, 18, 20

legs 10

mouth 12

paws 14, 18

range 6

roar 12

size 8

speed 10

teeth 12, 18

Visit **abdokids.com** to access crafts, games, videos, and more!

Use Abdo Kids code

ISK6363

or scan this QR code!